ARE 4.0

Programming, Planning & Practice

QUESTIONS & ANSWERS John Hardt

This publication is designed to provide accurate and authoritative information in regard to the subject matter covered. It is sold with the understanding that the publisher is not engaged in rendering legal, accounting, or other professional service. If legal advice or other expert assistance is required, the services of a competent professional should be sought.

President: Mehul Patel
Vice President & General Manager: David Dufresne
Vice President of Product Development and Publishing: Evan M. Butterfield
Editorial Project Manager: Jason Mitchell
Director of Production: Daniel Frey
Production Editor: Caitlin Ostrow
Production Artist: Virginia Byrne
Creative Director: Lucy Jenkins
Senior Product Manager: Brian O'Connor

Published by Kaplan AEC Education
30 South Wacker Drive, Suite 2500
Chicago, Illinois 60606-7481
(312) 836-4400
www.kaplanaecarchitecture.com

Printed in the United States of America

08   09   10   10   9   8   7   6   5   4   3   2

ISBN-13: 978-1-4277-7033-2
ISBN-10:   1-4277-7033-6

CONTENTS

WELCOME

Thank you for choosing Kaplan AEC Education for your ARE study needs. We offer updates annually to keep abreast of code and exam changes and to address any errors discovered since the previous update was published. We wish you the best of luck in your pursuit of licensure.

ARE OVERVIEW

Since the State of Illinois first pioneered the practice of licensing architects in 1897, architectural licensing has been increasingly adopted as a means to protect the public health, safety, and welfare. Today, all U.S. states and Canadian provinces require licensing for individuals practicing architecture. Licensing requirements vary by jurisdiction; however, the minimum requirements are uniform and in all cases include passing the Architect Registration Exam (ARE). This makes the ARE a required rite of passage for all those entering the profession, and you should be congratulated on undertaking this challenging endeavor.

Developed by the National Council of Architectural Registration Boards (NCARB), the ARE is the only exam by which architecture candidates can become registered in the United States or Canada. The ARE assesses candidates' knowledge, skills, and abilities in seven different areas of professional practice, including a candidate's competency in decision making and knowledge of various areas of the profession. The exam also tests competence in fulfilling an architect's responsibilities and in coordinating the activities of others while working with a team of design and construction specialists. In all jurisdictions, candidates must pass the seven divisions of the exam to become registered.

The ARE is designed and prepared by architects, making it a practice-based exam. It is generally not a test of academic knowledge, but rather a means to test decision-making ability as it relates to the responsibilities of the architectural profession. For example, the exam does not expect candidates to memorize specific details of the building code, but requires them to understand a model code's general requirements, scope, and purpose, and to know the architect's responsibilities related to that code. As such, there is no substitute for a well-rounded internship to help prepare for the ARE.

4.0 Exam Format

The seven ARE 4.0 divisions are outlined in the table below.

DIVISION	QUESTIONS	VIGNETTES
Building Design & Construction Systems	85	Accessibility/Ramp Roof Plan Stair Design
Building Systems	95	Mechanical & Electrical Plan
Construction Documents & Services	100	Building Section
Programming, Planning & Practice	85	Site Zoning
Schematic Design	-	Building Layout Interior Layout
Site Planning & Design	65	Site Design Site Grading
Structural Systems	125	Structural Layout

The exam presents multiple-choice questions individually. Candidates may answer questions, skip questions, or mark questions for further review. Candidates may also move backward or forward within the exam using

ARCHITECTURAL HISTORY

Questions pertaining to the history of architecture appear throughout the ARE. The prominence of historical questions will vary not only by division but also within different versions of the exam for each division. In general, however, history tends to be lightly tested, with approximately three to seven history questions per division, depending upon the total number of questions within the division. One aspect common to all the divisions is that whatever history questions are presented will be related to that division's subject matter. For example, a question regarding Chicago's John Hancock Center and the purpose of its unique exterior cross bracing may appear on the Structural Systems exam.

Though it is difficult to predict how essential your knowledge of architectural history will be to passing any of the multiple-choice divisions, it is recommended that you refer to a primer in this field—such as Kaplan's *Architectural History*—before taking each exam, and that you keep an eye out for topics relevant to the division for which you are studying. It is always better to be overprepared than taken by surprise at the testing center.

simple on-screen icons. The vignettes require candidates to create a graphic solution according to program and code requirements.

Actual appointment times for taking the exam are slightly longer than the actual exam time, allowing candidates to check in and out of the testing center. All ARE candidates are encouraged to review NCARB's *ARE Guidelines* for further detail about the exam format. These guidelines are available via free download at NCARB's Web site (*www.ncarb.org*).

Exam Format

It is important for exam candidates to familiarize themselves not only with exam content, but also with question format. Familiarity with the basic question types found in the ARE will reduce confusion, save time, and help you pass the exam. The ARE contains three basic questions types.

The first and most common type is a straightforward multiple-choice question followed by four choices (A, B, C, and D). Candidates are expected to select the correct answer. This type of question is shown in the following example.

Which of the following cities is the capital of the United States?

A. New York
B. Washington, DC
C. Chicago
D. Los Angeles

The second type of question is a negatively worded question. In questions such as this, the negative wording is usually highlighted using all caps, as shown below.

Which of the following cities is NOT located on the west coast of the United States?

A. Los Angeles
B. San Diego
C. San Francisco
D. New York

The third type of question is a combination question. In a combination question, more than one choice may be correct; candidates must select from combinations of potentially correct choices. An example of a combination question is shown on page viii.

THE EXAM TRANSITION

ARE 3.1

In November 2005 NCARB released *ARE Guidelines* Version 3.1, which outlines changes to the exam effective February 2006. These guidelines primarily detailed changes for the Site Planning division, combining the site design and site parking vignettes as well as the site zoning and site analysis vignettes. For more details about these changes, please refer to Kaplan's study guides for the graphic divisions.

The guidelines mean less to those preparing for multiple-choice divisions. Noteworthy points are outlined below.

- All division statements and content area descriptions were unchanged for the multiple-choice divisions.

- The number of questions and time limits for all exams were unchanged.

- The list of codes and standards candidates should familiarize themselves with was reduced to those of the International Code Council (ICC), the National Fire Protection Association (NFPA), and the National Research Council of Canada.

- A statics title has been removed from the reference list for General Structures.

ARE 4.0

In the spring of 2007, NCARB unveiled ARE 4.0, available as of July 2008. According to NCARB, the 4.0 version of the exam will be more subject-oriented than 3.1, and is intended to better assess a candidate's ability to approach projects independently. The format combines the multiple-choice and graphic portions of different divisions, reducing the number of divisions from nine to seven.

The transition will be gradual, with a one-year overlap during which both ARE 3.1 and ARE 4.0 will be administered. Provided you pass at least one ARE 3.1 division prior to May 2008, you can continue to take ARE 3.1 divisions until July 2009.

If you have not passed all ARE 3.1 divisions by June 2009, you will be transitioned to the ARE 4.0 format. You will be given credit for ARE 4.0 divisions according to which 3.1 divisions you have passed. Visit *www.kaplanaecarchitecture.com* for more details.

In order to avoid being retested on subjects you have already passed, you should develop a strategy for which divisions you take in which order. Here are some key points to keep in mind:

- Building Technology is a key division in the transition; its vignettes will be dispersed across four ARE 4.0 divisions. Be sure to pass Building Technology if you have passed and want credit for any of the following ARE 3.1 divisions: Building Design/Materials & Methods; Construction Documents & Services; General Structures; Lateral Forces; or Mechanical & Electrical Systems.

- Pre-Design and Site Planning content will be shuffled in ARE 4.0: If you pass one, pass the other.

- General Structures, Lateral Forces, and the Structural Layout vignette from Building Technology are being merged into the Structural Systems division. If you pass any of these and want to avoid being retested on material you have already seen, pass all three.

Which of the following cities are located within the United States?

    I. New York

    II. Toronto

    III. Montreal

    IV. Los Angeles

A. I only

B. I and II

C. II and III

D. I and IV

The single most important thing candidates can do to prepare themselves for the vignettes is to learn to proficiently navigate NCARB's graphic software. Practice software can be downloaded free of charge from their Web site. Candidates should download it and become thoroughly familiar with its use.

Recommendations on Exam Division Order

NCARB allows candidates to choose the order in which they take the exams, and the choice is an important one. While only you know what works best for you, the following are some general considerations that many have found to be beneficial:

1. The Building Design & Construction Systems and Programming, Planning & Practice divisions are perhaps the broadest of all the divisions. Although this can make them among the most intimidating, taking these divisions early in the process will give a candidate a broad base of knowledge and may prove helpful in preparing for subsequent divisions. An alternative to this approach is to take these two divisions last, since you will already be familiar with much of their content. This latter approach likely is most beneficial when you take the exam divisions in fairly rapid succession so that details learned while studying for earlier divisions will still be fresh in your mind.

2. The Construction Documents & Services exam covers a broad range of subjects, dealing primarily with the architect's role and responsibilities within the building design and construction team. Because these subjects serve as one of the core foundations of the ARE, it may be advisable to take this division early in the process, as knowledge gained preparing for this exam can help in subsequent divisions.

3. Take exams that particularly concern you early in the process. NCARB rules prohibit retaking an exam for six months. Therefore, failing an exam early in the process will allow the candidate to use the waiting period to prepare for and take other exams.

EXAM PREPARATION

Overview

There is little argument that preparation is key to passing the ARE. With this in mind, Kaplan has developed a complete learning system for each exam division, including study guides, question-and-answer handbooks, mock exams, and flash cards. The study guides offer a condensed course of study and will best prepare you for the exam when utilized along with the other tools in the learning system. The system is designed to provide you with the general background necessary to pass the exam and to provide an indication of specific content areas that demand additional attention.

In addition to the Kaplan learning system, materials from industry-standard documents may prove useful for the various divisions. Several of these sources are noted in the "Supplementary Study Materials" section below.

Understanding the Exam

The Programming, Planning & Practice exam is among the most broad of all the ARE divisions. The exam content spans a wide range of topics including city planning, programming, space needs, land development and site planning, code, financing, geology and soils zoning, project management, interaction among the design team, project delivery methods, practice of architecture, budgeting and cost estimating, accessibility, and building layout. Further, environmental, social, and economic issues as well as sustainability are all subject matters for which the candidate should prepare.

Although the exam content is diverse, the material is all related to the pre-design process and many of the aforementioned topics overlap. Since many of the subjects covered span other exam divisions, this exam is widely considered one of the more difficult for which to prepare. However, the exam tends to focus on general principles of the above issues and avoids detailed calculations and data. For the Site Zoning vignette, remember not to disturb existing trees, to use the sketch lines, and to align driveways properly. Also be sure to use the zoom, full screen cursor, and background grid to produce more accurate solutions.

Preparation Basics

The first step in preparation should be a review of the exam specifications and reference materials published by NCARB. These statements are available for each of the seven ARE divisions to serve as a guide for preparing for the exam. Download these statements and familiarize yourself with their content. This will help you focus your attention on the subjects on which the exam focuses.

Prior CAD knowledge is not necessary to successfully complete vignettes. In fact, it's important for candidates familiar with CAD to

realize they will experience significant differences between CAD and the drawing tools used on the exam.

Though no two people will have exactly the same ARE experience, the following are recommended best practices to adopt in your studies and should serve as a guide.

Set aside scheduled study time.
Establish a routine and adopt study strategies that reflect your strengths and mirror your approach in other successful academic pursuits. Most importantly, set aside a definite amount of study time each week, just as if you were taking a lecture course, and carefully read all of the material.

Take—and retake—quizzes.
After studying each lesson in the study guide, take the quiz found at its conclusion. The quiz questions are intended to be straightforward and objective. Answers and explanations can be found at the back of the book. If you answer a question incorrectly, see if you can determine why the correct answer is correct before reading the explanation. Retake the quiz until you answer every question correctly and understand why the correct answers are correct.

Identify areas for improvement.
The quizzes allow you the opportunity to pinpoint areas where you need improvement. Reread and take note of the sections that cover these areas and seek additional information from other sources. Use the question-and-answer handbook and online test bank as a final tune-up for the exam.

Take the final exam.
A final exam designed to simulate the ARE follows the last lesson of each study guide. Answers and explanations can be found on the pages following the exam. As with the lesson quizzes, retake the final exam until you answer

every question correctly and understand why the correct answers are correct.

Use the flash cards.

If you've purchased the flash cards, go through them once and set aside any terms you know at first glance. Take the rest to work, reviewing them on the train, over lunch, or before bed. Remove cards as you become familiar with their terms until you know all the terms. Review all the cards a final time before taking the exam.

Practice using the NCARB software.

Work through the practice vignettes contained within the NCARB software. You should work through each vignette repeatedly until you can solve it easily. As your skills develop, track how long it takes to work through a solution for each vignette.

Supplementary Study Materials

In addition to the Kaplan learning system, materials from industry-standard sources may prove useful in your studies. Candidates should consult the list of exam references in the NCARB guidelines for the council's recommendations and pay particular attention to the following publications, which are essential to successfully completing this exam:

- International Code Council (ICC) *International Building Code*
- American Institute of Architects B141-1997 *Standard Form of Agreement Between Owner and Architect*
- American Institute of Architects A201-1997 *General Conditions of the Contract for Construction*

Test-Taking Advice

Preparation for the exam should include a review of successful test-taking procedures—especially for those who have been out of the classroom for some time. Following is advice to aid in your success.

Pace yourself.

Each division allows candidates at least one minute per question. You should be able to comfortably read and reread each question and fully understand what is being asked before answering. Each vignette allows candidates ample time to complete a solution within the time allotted.

Read carefully.

Begin each question by reading it carefully and fully reviewing the choices, eliminating those that are obviously incorrect. Interpret language literally, and keep an eye out for negatively worded questions. With vignettes, carefully review instructions and requirements. Quickly make a list of program and code requirements to check your work against as you proceed through the vignette.

Guess.

All unanswered questions are considered incorrect, so answer every question. If you are unsure of the correct answer, select your best guess and/or mark the question for later review. If you continue to be unsure of the answer after returning the question a second time, it is usually best to stick with your first guess.

Review difficult questions.

The exam allows candidates to review and change answers within the time limit. Utilize this feature to mark troubling questions for review upon completing the rest of the exam.

Reference material.

Some divisions include reference materials accessible through an on-screen icon. These materials include formulas and other reference content that may prove helpful when answering questions in these divisions. Note that candidates may *not* bring reference material with them to the testing center.

Best answer questions.

Many candidates fall victim to questions seeking the "best" answer. In these cases, it may appear at first glance as though several choices are correct. Remember the importance of reviewing the question carefully and interpreting the language literally. Consider the following example.

> Which of these cities is located on the east coast of the United States?
>
> **A.** Boston
>
> **B.** Philadelphia
>
> **C.** Washington, DC
>
> **D.** Atlanta

At first glance, it may appear that all of the cities could be correct answers. However, if you interpret the question literally, you'll identify the critical phrase as "on the east coast." Although each of the cities listed is arguably an "eastern" city, only Boston sits on the Atlantic coast. All the other choices are located in the eastern part of the country, but are not coastal cities.

Style doesn't count.

Vignettes are graded on their conformance with program requirements and instructions. Don't waste time creating aesthetically pleasing solutions and adding unnecessary design elements.

ACKNOWLEDGMENTS

This introduction was written by John F. Hardt, AIA. Mr. Hardt is vice president and senior project architect with Karlsberger, an architecture, planning, and design firm based in Columbus, Ohio. He is a graduate of Ohio State University (MArch).

ABOUT KAPLAN

Thank you for choosing Kaplan AEC Education as your source for ARE preparation materials. Whether helping future professors prepare for the GRE or providing tomorrow's doctors the tools they need to pass the MCAT, Kaplan possesses more than 50 years of experience as a global leader in exam prep and educational publishing. It is that experience and history that Kaplan brings to the world of architectural education, pairing unparalleled resources with acknowledged experts in ARE content areas to bring you the very best in licensure study materials.

Only Kaplan AEC offers a complete catalog of individual products and integrated learning systems to help you pass all seven divisions of the ARE. Kaplan's ARE materials include study guides, mock exams, question-and-answer handbooks, video workshops, and flash cards. Products may be purchased individually or in division-specific learning systems to suit your needs. These systems are designed to help you better focus on essential information for each division, provide flexibility in how you study, and save you money.

To order, please visit *www.KaplanAEC.com* or call (800) 420-1429.

SYMBOLS & ABBREVIATIONS

The following symbols and abbreviations are used in this book and are generally understood in structural design practice.

Symbol or Abbreviation	Meaning
ft. or '	foot
ft^2 or sq. ft.	square foot
ft^3 or cu. ft.	cubic foot
ft.-kip or ft.-k or 'k	foot-kip
ft.-lb. or ft-# or '#	foot-pound
in. or "	inch
in^2 or sq. in.	square inch
in^3 or cu. in.	cubic inch
in.-kip. or in.-k or "k	inch-kip
in.-lb. or in-# or "#	inch-pound
kip or k	kip (1 kip = 1 kilo pound or 1,000 pounds)
ksi or k/in^2	kips per square inch
lb. or #	pound
lb./cu. ft. or $\#/ft^3$ or pcf	pounds per cubic foot
plf or #/' or #/ft.	pounds per lineal foot
psf or $\#/ft^2$	pounds per square foot
psi or $\#/in^2$	pounds per square inch
Δ (delta)	1. total strain (deformation)
	2. thermal expansion or contraction
	3. deflection
θ (theta)	a common designation for an angle
π (pi)	the ratio of the circumference of a circle toits diameter, equal to 3.14159
Σ (sigma)	summation of
φ (phi)	strength reduction factor in reinforced concrete design
#	pounds

1. The design of a two-story senior citizen center includes, as its largest space, a multi-purpose meeting hall that seats 300 people. It is anticipated that this meeting facility will be used frequently. Where should it be located within the building? Check all that apply.

    A. At the extreme end of the structure, for easy exiting

    B. On the second level of the structure, for privacy

    C. Near the structure's ground floor entrance

    D. At the side of the structure with the best view

    E. Within easy access of the toilet rooms

2. The chief goal in creating an architectural program is to

    A. establish the project intent.

    B. identify the nature of the problem.

    C. organize the project standards.

    D. determine the project form.

3. A second mortgage on a piece of property generally carries a higher interest rate because the mortgagee

    A. has no right of foreclosure on the property.

    B. may have greater difficulty in obtaining repayment.

    C. is usually an individual rather than an institution.

    D. is not bound by the normal regulations concerning usury.

4. A hospital cafeteria is designed to serve doctors, nurses, and visitors. An important planning goal of the hospital administration is maximum flexibility, economy, and comfort. Which among the following seating arrangements best expresses the client's goal?

    A. Individual counter seating

    B. Two-person rectangular tables

    C. Four-person round tables

    D. Four-person booths

5. Which of the following features is not associated with the John Hancock Building in Chicago?

    A. Distinctive x-bracing structure

    B. Park-like setting

    C. Open ground floor shopping plaza

    D. Battered tower inclines inward as it rises

6. The programmed efficiency of a building is 65 percent. If the efficiency were increased to 70 percent and the net area remained constant, the gross area would

    A. decrease by 7 percent.

    B. decrease by 5 percent.

    C. remain unchanged.

    D. increase by 5 percent.

7. The well-decomposed, more or less stable part of the organic matter found in mineral soils is _____.

8. The project development budget for a proposed County Library is limited to 6.3 million dollars. The building program results in a total net usable area of 49,000 square feet with a targeted efficiency of 70 percent. Select the incorrect statement from those below.

   A. The total gross building area will be 70,000 square feet.

   B. The unit cost for construction will be $90 per square foot.

   C. At 8 percent the architect's fee would not exceed $500,000.

   D. The cost of furnishings and equipment would normally be included in the 6.3 million dollar budget.

9. A lecture hall is programmed to accommodate 300 persons in fixed auditorium-type seats. A demonstration table with sink and utilities and the adjacent lecture area requires approximately 500 square feet. Which of the following dimensions would provide an adequate space for the programmed use?

   A. 50 feet wide by 50 feet deep

   B. 40 feet wide by 65 feet deep

   C. 50 feet wide by 80 feet deep

   D. 25 feet wide by 110 feet deep

10. A graphic representation of the relationships of spaces is called a

   _____.

11. Which of the following schematic diagrams of a hypothetical office structure allows the most direct elevator access from any point on the ground floor to the upper floors of the tower?

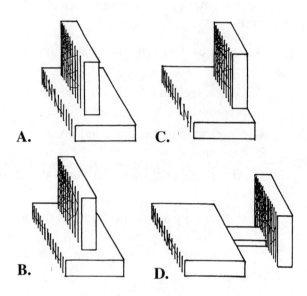

A.   C.

B.   D.

12. Diagrammatic layouts, also referred to as concept or bubble diagrams, graphically represent which of the following?

   I.   Floor area comparisons
   II.   Circulation relationships
   III. Structural considerations
   IV.   Physical configurations
   V.   Functional associations

   A. I and II

   B. II and V

   C. I, III, and V

   D. I, IV, and V

13. The following schematic designs represent a typical floor of a multistory apartment building located along a body of water. Which design would best accomplish the objective of providing a view of the water? Assume an equal number of units in each design.

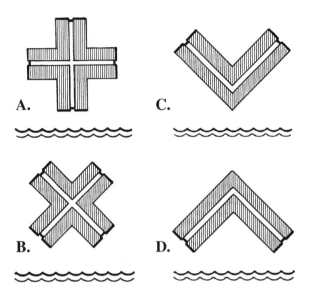

A.

B.

C.

D.

14. Which of the following statements about programming and design are correct?

   I.   Programming is problem seeking, while design is problem solving.

   II.   Programming involves physical solutions to architectural problems.

   III.   Design involves functional solutions to performance problems.

   IV.   Ideally, programming should be completed before design is begun.

   A. II and III

   B. I, II, and III

   C. I and IV

   D. I, II, III, and IV

15. The maximum allowable floor area ratio for the lot shown is 2.0. Which of the following statements is correct?

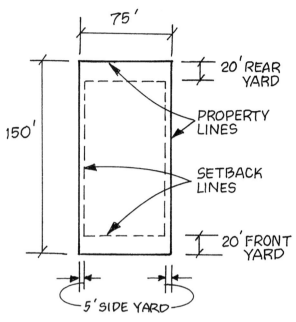

   A. The total floor area of a building on this lot may not exceed 5,625 square feet.

   B. The total floor area of a building on this lot may not exceed 14,300 square feet.

   C. The total floor area of a building on this lot may not exceed 22,500 square feet.

   D. The net floor area of a building on this lot may not exceed 22,500 square feet.

16. Other than the building program, which of the following would have the greatest impact on the floor area of a building?

   A. Site utilities

   B. Topography

   C. Functional relationships

   D. Building codes

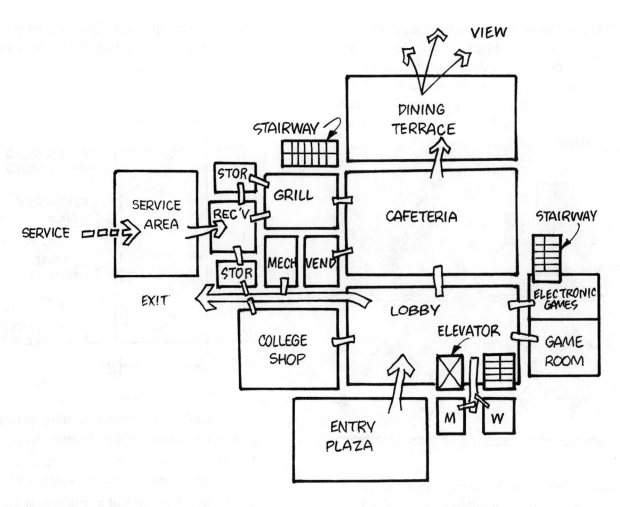

17. With reference to the diagrammatic layout shown, an exit path from the cafeteria might go through any of the following spaces, *EXCEPT* the

A. lobby/entry plaza.

B. dining terrace.

C. lobby/exit corridor.

D. electronic games.

18. An assessment made according to the value of a property is called _____.

19. Mannerism is an architectural style that may be accurately described as

A. an expression in which classic elements are used unconventionally.

B. an expression in which classic motifs are harmoniously integrated.

C. the expression most frequently used by postmodernist architects.

D. the expression most closely identified with Charles Moore.

20. The cluster-type residential development would be most appropriate for an area that has

    A. a restricted size.

    B. dense natural foliage.

    C. unusually high fuel costs.

    D. highly irregular contours.

21. The City Beautiful Movement from the 1890s resulted in all of the following, *EXCEPT*

    A. it restored human scale to the new industrial cities.

    B. it launched a classic revival moment throughout the country.

    C. it led to a greater awareness of city planning.

    D. it resulted in a profusion of dome-topped civic buildings.

22. Which of the following traffic circulation systems might be considered the best choice for a community focused on sustainable design?

    A. Curvilinear system

    B. Grid system

    C. Radial system

    D. Linear system

23. The geographic area from which the customers of a retail center are drawn is called a _____.

24. Which of the following statements about landscaping is *NOT* correct?

    A. Trees can be used to screen winds and increase ventilation in desired areas.

    B. Vegetation can capture moisture, reduce fog, and increase the amount of sunlight reaching the ground.

    C. Coniferous trees screen out direct sunlight in the summer while allowing it to pass in the winter.

    D. Planted areas are cooler during hot days and have less heat loss during the night.

25. To discourage vandalism in a housing project, which of the following details should be incorporated at exterior spaces?

    A. Exterior paths and entrance doors arranged for visibility

    B. Exterior paths arranged in curves, rather than straight lines

    C. Low levels of exterior lighting to eliminate glare

    D. Natural and attractive exterior materials used to inspire respect

26. If a designer wanted to impart symbolic importance to a public institutional building, the form of the structure might include

    I.   a number of wide entrance doors.

    II. a symmetrical arrangement.

    III. a long flight of entrance steps.

    IV. small, randomly placed windows.

    V. a flagpole.

    A. I, II, and V   **C.** II, III, and V

    B. I, III, and V   **D.** II, III, and IV

27. If a building were to be planned with regard to the sun's impact on space heating, the most desirable forms of the building would be which of the following?

    I.   Circular

    II. Square

    III. Elongated on the north-south axis

    IV. Staggered vertically or horizontally

    V. Stacked vertically

    A. I and III

    B. IV and V

    C. I, II, and IV

    D. II, III, IV, and V

28. Kevin Lynch described five basic elements that comprise one's perception of a city. The Harvard campus in Cambridge, Massachusetts, is an example of which element?

    A. Path

    B. District

    C. Landmark

    D. Node

29. If you were commissioned to restore a 19th-century building designed in the Second Empire Style, you might have to consider

    I.   a mansard roof.

    II. accents of color.

    III. forward breaks in elevation.

    IV. multiple towers.

    A. II and IV

    B. I and II

    C. I and III

    D. III and IV

30. A five-story reinforced concrete office building is planned for a site. A soil boring log for the site is shown below. Which of the following foundation types is likely to be economical and appropriate?

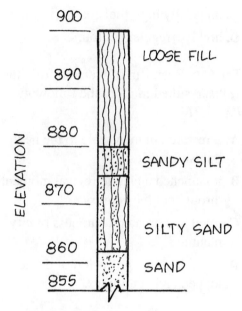

    A. Grade beams on piles

    B. Spread footings

    C. Spread footings on recompacted fill

    D. Mat foundation

31. Symmetry in architectural design is associated with which of the following?

    I.   Formality

    II. Uncomplicated building programs

    III. Authority

    IV. Irregular building sites

    A. I and III

    B. I, II, and III

    C. II and III

    D. I and IV

32. Which of the following site planning techniques are most effective in inhibiting criminal activity in a residential community?

    I. Large superblocks with no interior vehicular traffic

    II. Sites subdivided by streets

    III. Symbolic barriers that define the boundaries of a site

    IV. Play areas located at the periphery of a site

    A. I only

    B. II and III

    C. II and IV

    D. I and III

33. Which of the building forms shown is the most appropriate for a temperate climate?

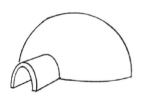 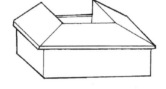

A.   **C.**

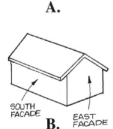 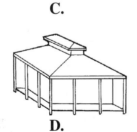

B.   **D.**

34. What is the floor area ratio (FAR) of a five-story building on a one-acre parcel of land, if each floor contains 17,420 square feet?

    A. One

    B. Two

    C. Three

    D. Five

35. The Natural Step is an approach to the environment that follows which of the following principles?

    I. The biosphere affecting humans is a relatively stable and resilient zone that includes five miles into the earth's crust and five miles into the atmosphere.

    II. Improved technologies have dramatically increased the number and quantity of available natural resources.

    III. Toxic substances released into either the sea or atmosphere will only influence areas adjacent to the toxic source.

    IV. Using building materials that are recycled is an adequate sustainable design approach.

    A. I

    B. II

    C. II and IV

    D. None of the above

36. Select the *INCORRECT* statement about life-cycle cost.

    A. Financing costs may be decreased when a fast-track procedure is used.

    B. Construction costs represent about 15 percent of the long-term cost of a project.

    C. High quality products usually have a greater long-term cost than products of lower quality.

    D. Life-cycle costs include the costs of replacement and renovation.

37. Which of the following are included in the federal guidelines for rehabilitating buildings on the National Register of Historic Places? Check all that apply.

    A. Every reasonable effort shall be made to use a property for its originally intended purpose or to provide a compatible use that requires minimum alteration of the building's structure, site, and environment.

    B. Changes that have taken place in the course of time may have acquired significance in their own right, and this significance shall be recognized and respected.

    C. Deteriorated architectural features shall be replaced rather than repaired, wherever possible, with materials that match the design, color, texture, and other visual qualities of the original materials.

    D. Contemporary design for alterations to existing properties shall not be discouraged when such alterations are compatible and do not destroy significant historical, architectural, or cultural material.

38. The total width of exits required for a multistory building is determined by the

    A. the occupant load of the largest floor in the building.

    B. the total number of occupants in the building.

    C. the area of the largest floor in the building.

    D. the purpose for which the building is used.

39. The International Building Code classifies every building according to which two of the following?

    I. The building's quality of construction

    II. The building's type of construction

    III. The building's occupancy

    IV. The building's proximity to fire department equipment

    A. I and II

    B. I and III

    C. II and III

    D. II and IV

40. Which of the following statements would least likely be found in the building code?

    A. Stairs in smokeproof enclosures shall be of noncombustible construction.

    B. No leaf of an exit door shall exceed four feet in width.

    C. The maximum height and number of stories of a building shall be dependent on its occupancy and type of construction.

    D. The area of the building may not exceed 75 percent of the total area of the building lot.

41. The goal of barrier-free design is to

    A. permit autonomous functioning.

    B. permit free use by the nonambulatory.

    C. eliminate the physical barriers within all buildings.

    D. provide unobstructed access to all buildings.

42. Select the statement that is *LEAST* correct.

    A. Barrier-free design is frequently considered to be a civil right.

    B. Barrier-free design is usually beneficial to all building users.

    C. Barrier-free design resolves the life safety problems of the handicapped.

    D. Barrier-free design generally increases a project's cost.

43. In a public building it is necessary to provide an appropriate number of public telephones that are accessible to physically handicapped persons. In this regard, which of the following considerations must be taken into account?

    I. Locate the phones on the ground floor

    II. Height of the coin slot

    III. Size of doors leading to the phones

    IV. Provisions for hearing disabilities

    V. Visual identification sign

    A. I, II, and III

    B. III, IV, and V

    C. I, II, and V

    D. II, III, IV, and V

44. A knurled door knob would be of greatest benefit to someone who is

    A. blind.

    B. arthritic.

    C. confined to a wheelchair.

    D. using crutches.

45. In general, why does a governmental agency use the right of eminent domain?

    I. To acquire land from an owner who refuses to sell at any price

    II. To acquire land from an owner who refuses to accept the purchase price offered by the agency

    III. To establish a scale of values, which is then used to determine fair compensation for all owners whose property is acquired

    IV. To avoid the normal procedures for buying land, which are costly and time-consuming

    V. To avoid a court determination of the value of acquired land

    A. I, II, and IV

    B. I and II

    C. I, III, and V

    D. II, IV, and V

46. Zoning ordinances provide light, air, and spaciousness through the use of

_____.

47. An urban site is 130 feet wide in an area where the zoning ordinance requires the minimum to be 150 feet. Under these circumstances, the owner wishing to develop the site would probably apply for

    A. spot zoning.

    B. incentive zoning.

    C. a conditional use permit.

    D. a zoning variance.

48. The zoning ordinance requires 6-foot side yards in a residential zone. However, overhanging eaves are permitted to project a maximum of 18 inches into the side yards. If a building has a 6-foot overhanging eave, how close to the side property line can the building be placed?

A. 6 feet

B. 7 feet 6 inches

C. 10 feet 6 inches

D. 12 feet

51. An acquired right of use by one party on the property of another without ownership is called a(n) _____.

52. According to the International Building Code (IBC), an office building that is designated Use Group B (Business) and being constructed of Type IV construction is permitted to have what maximum height and area? Use the table provided.

		TYPES OF CONSTRUCTION								
		I	II			III		IV	V	
		F.R.	F.R.	One-hour	N	One-hour	N	H.T.	One-hour	N
TYPE OF CONSTRUCTION	Height	UL	160 (48 768 mm)	65 (19 812 mm)	55 (16 764 mm)	65 (19 812 mm)	55 (16 764 mm)	65 (19 812 mm)	50 (15 240 mm)	40 (12 192 mm)
Use Group	Height				× 0.0929 for m²					
A-1	H	UL	4	Not Permitted						
	A	UL	29,900							
A-2, 2.1²	H	UL	4	2	NP	2	NP	2	2	NP
	A	UL	29,900	13,500	NP	13,500	NP	13,500	10,500	NP
A-3, 4²	H	UL	12	2	1	2	1	2	2	1
	A	UL	29,900	13,500	9,100	13,500	9,100	13,500	10,500	6,100
B, F-1, M, S-1, S-3, S-5	H	UL	12	4	2	4	2	4	3	2
	A	UL	39,900	18,000	12,000	18,000	12,000	18,000	14,000	8,000
E-1, 2, 3⁴	H	UL	4	2	1	2	1	2	2	1
	A	UL	45,200	20,200	13,500	20,200	13,500	20,200	15,700	9,100
F-2, S-2³	H	UL	12	4	2	4	2	4	3	2
	A	UL	59,900	27,000	18,000	27,000	18,000	27,000	21,000	12,000
H-1⁵	H	1	1	1	1	Not Permitted				
	A	15,000	12,400	5,600	3,700					
H-2⁵	H	UL	2	1	1	1	1	1	1	1
	A	15,000	12,400	5,600	3,700	5,600	3,700	5,600	4,400	2,500
H-3, 4, 5⁵	H	UL	5	2	1	2	1	2	2	1
	A	UL	24,800	11,200	7,500	11,200	7,500	11,200	8,800	5,100
H-6, 7	H	3	3	3	2	3	2	3	3	1
	A	UL	39,900	18,000	12,000	18,000	12,000	18,000	14,000	8,000
I-1.1⁶, 1.2	H	UL	3	1	NP	1	NP	1	1	NP
	A	UL	15,100	6,800	NP	6,800	NP	6,800	5,200	NP
I-2	H	UL	3	2	NP	2	NP	2	2	NP
	A	UL	15,100	6,800	NP	6,800	NP	6,800	5,200	NP
I-3	H	UL	2	Not Permitted⁷						
	A	UL	15,100							
R-1	H	UL	12	4	2⁹	4	2⁹	5	3	2⁹
	A	UL	29,900	13,500	9,100⁹	13,500	9,100⁹	13,500	10,500	6,000⁹

49. The designation of a parcel of land for a use classification different from that of the surrounding area to favor a particular owner is called _____.

50. Special permission granted to an owner to deviate from the zoning requirements normally applicable to his property is called

A. spot zoning.

B. variance.

C. conditional use.

D. nonconforming use.

A. One story and 12,000 square feet per floor

B. Two stories and 12,000 square feet per floor

C. Two stories and 18,000 square feet per floor

D. Four stories and 18,000 square feet per floor

53. The occupancy classification, or Use Group, of a structure is determined by the activities for which the structure is intended. Which of the following is *NOT* an occupancy classification recognized by the International Building Code (IBC)?

    A. Business (B)
    B. Institutional (I)
    C. Assembly (A)
    D. Office (O)

54. Which of the following is the *PRIMARY* purpose of the fire resistance requirements in the International Building Code (IBC)?

    A. Maintain structural integrity long enough for firefighters to extinguish the blaze
    B. Provide sufficient protection to the structure to limit damage and avoid collapse
    C. Permit the safe egress of the occupants in the event of fire
    D. Protect the contents of the structure

55. To encourage openness, some zoning codes limit the bulk of a building by means of a formula that restricts the total floor area to a multiple of the lot area. This is referred to as the

    A. allowable floor area.
    B. floor area ratio.
    C. required yards.
    D. maximum lot coverage.

56. The critical factor in determining the size of building exits is the occupant load of the building. This calculation is determined by using

    A. requirements specified in the building code.
    B. the number of occupants the architect expects to utilize the building.
    C. the expected number of occupants as established by the owner.
    D. the number of occupants expected to use the building based on precedent.

57. Stairways that serve as required building exits must meet numerous requirements described in the code. Among these are

    I.   width, rise, and run of the steps.
    II. location of the handrails.
    III. headroom.
    IV. fire rating of the enclosure.
    A. I and II
    B. I, II, and III
    C. I, II, and IV
    D. I, II, III, and IV

58. In the critical path network diagram shown, which of the following is the critical path?

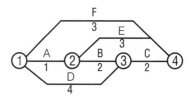

    A. 1-4
    B. 1-3-4
    C. 1-2-4
    D. 1-2-3-4

59. Float time is

A. the amount of time that a construction activity can be delayed without causing the project completion to be delayed.

B. the amount of time between completion of an increment of construction and the earliest date when loads may safely be imposed on that increment.

C. nonproductive time on a construction project, such as weekends and holidays.

D. the shortest time required to complete a construction activity.

60. A $100 per student per semester fee is the principal source of revenue to repay a proposed bond issue for the planned construction of a new student union to be located on a state college campus. Based on the college's preliminary assessment of space needs, the project cost will exceed the proposed bond issue by approximately 25 percent. In response to the owner's request for guidance, the architect would most likely recommend which of the following?

A. Increase the student fee to $125 per semester and proceed with the project.

B. Delay the project until the student enrollment has increased to the point where it can support the larger bond issue required for the project.

C. Proceed with the project on the basis of the available funds and attempt to reduce the scope or quality of work during the programming phase.

D. Request the owner to reduce his gross space needs sufficiently to meet the budgetary constraints prior to entering into an agreement for professional services.

61. That portion of a construction loan that must be paid to the lender for the privilege of borrowing the money is called the

A. discount.

B. recording fee.

C. balloon payment.

D. amortization.

62. Select the correct statements about the critical path method (CPM).

I. The path in the network diagram that has the longest total required time is called the critical path.

II. The extra time available for an activity is called the float.

III. CPM utilizes bar graphs to show the sequential relationships between construction activities.

A. I and II

B. II and III

C. I and III

D. I, II, and III

63. A system of planning construction operations that analyzes sequences and durations of time using network diagrams is called

A. bar graph.

B. scheduling.

C. critical path method.

D. project calendar.

64. Which of the following architectural services are *NOT* typically within the scope of an architect's basic services?

A. Programming

B. Schematic design

C. Design development

D. Construction documents

65. In the critical path network diagram shown, what is the critical path?

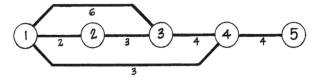

  A. 1-3-4-5

  B. 1-2-3-4-5

  C. 1-4-5

  D. 1-2-3-4

66. Which of the following has the *LEAST* impact on the time required for schematic design?

  A. The size and complexity of the project

  B. The quality and completeness of the program

  C. The decision-making ability of the client

  D. The size of the design team

67. Which of the following statements regarding float is *INCORRECT*?

  A. It is defined as difference in time duration between the critical path and any other path.

  B. It is a measure of the extra time available for a given activity or group of activities.

  C. As long as float time is not exceeded, no delay in project completion will result.

  D. Any activity may be delayed, so long as the delay does not exceed the available float.

68. Which of the following is a method by which a community might finance the construction of a new community recreation center?

  A. Comprehensive planning

  B. Property tax

  C. Bonds

  D. Eminent domain

69. An HVAC engineer would likely perform final cooling load calculations and perform detailed ductwork layouts in which phase of basic services?

  A. Pre-design

  B. Schematic design

  C. Design development

  D. Construction documentation

70. Buildings are often sited parallel, rather than perpendicular, to the contours because that orientation generally

  A. minimizes the amount of grading required to fit the building to the site.

  B. minimizes the amount of disturbance to the existing natural surface drainage.

  C. maximizes the available area for construction.

  D. maximizes the solar advantage in northern latitudes.

71. On a road with a gradient of 5 percent, what will the elevation be 150 feet distant and uphill from a point at elevation 142.5?

  A. 135

  B. 149.5

  C. 150

  D. 183.3

72. Where topography is steep and irregular, the installation of an underground sewer line is generally

 A. more expensive than for a level site, because the line requires more sewer manholes.

 B. less expensive than for a level site, because the line can follow the natural slope to drain.

 C. less expensive than for a level site, because the line will require less excavation.

 D. about the same expense as for a level site, because the underground work for both is similar.

73. Solid contour lines on a topographic map do which of the following?

 I. Connect points of equal elevation

 II. Represent proposed landform modifications

 III. Indicate natural topographic configurations

 IV. Never close on themselves

 V. Never split in two

 A. I and V

 B. III and IV

 C. I, II, and V

 D. I, II, IV, and V

74. All of the following information may be found on a topographic map, *EXCEPT*

 A. property lines, easements, and utilities.

 B. location of streams.

 C. location of roads and buildings.

 D. location and identification of soil conditions.

75. In the hot-arid climatic zone of the United States, which of the following construction elements would be appropriate?

 I. Thick walls

 II. Wide overhangs

 III. Dense windbreaks

 IV. High ceilings

 A. I and II

 B. I, II, and IV

 C. II, III, and IV

 D. I, III, and IV

76. The first winter after completion of a construction project, the building remained stable, but large paved areas of an adjacent parking lot rose several inches above their original level. The probable reason was because

 A. of frost and heaving of the subsoil.

 B. the parking lot was built over filled land.

 C. the paving subsurface was insufficiently compacted.

 D. a subsurface water or sewer pipe froze and burst.

77. On a topographic survey that has a contour interval of 1 foot, a road is shown with a 5 percent grade. How far apart will the contours on the road be indicated?

 A. 1 foot

 B. 2 feet

 C. 10 feet

 D. 20 feet

78. For the graded bank shown below, the grade of the slope is

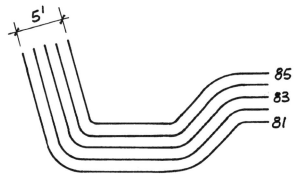

A. 12.5 percent

B. 40 percent

C. 80 percent

D. 125 percent

79. Vehicles entering a parking lot from the street generally have a different effective turning radius than vehicles exiting from the same lot. The reason for this is because

A. drivers entering a parking lot are usually less familiar with the lot layout than those exiting.

B. drivers entering a parking lot are usually moving at a faster rate than those exiting.

C. drivers entering a parking lot usually take less care than those exiting.

D. entrance driveways are usually wider than exit driveways, since it is assumed that those exiting have greater control than those entering.

80. Select the incorrect statement concerning traffic flow in a parking area.

A. Traffic aisles should be arranged so that they lead towards the buildings they serve.

B. Angled parking requires one-way traffic flow.

C. Perpendicular parking layouts usually lead to the most rapid traffic flow.

D. Circulation of traffic within large parking areas should be continuous.

81. The U.S. System of Surveying the Public Lands, begun in 1785, divides land into

A. townships and sections.

B. metes and bounds.

C. blocks and lots.

D. villages and hamlets.

82. A _____ is a legal clause that places limitations or restrictions on the use of the property.

83. Which of the following utility lines do *NOT* flow by gravity?

I.   Sanitary sewers

II.   Storm drains

III. Water lines

IV.   Gas lines

A. III only

B. I and IV

C. II, III, and IV

D. III and IV

84. The dotted line in the contour map shown represents a

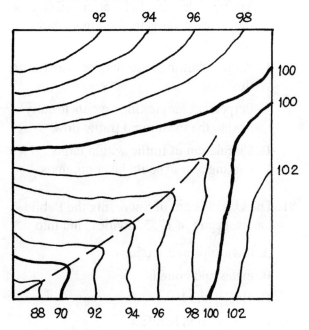

A. swale.

B. ridge.

C. trench drain.

D. drain pipe.

85. What is the grade of the slope shown?

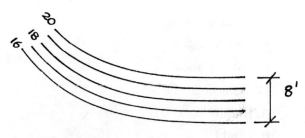

A. 20 percent

B. 40 percent

C. 50 percent

D. 100 percent

86. The contours shown below represent a

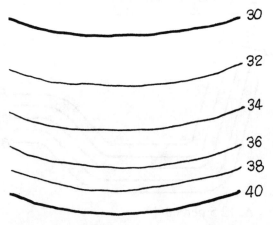

A. uniform slope.

B. concave slope.

C. convex slope.

D. valley.

87. Which of the following statements about septic drain fields is correct?

A. The underlying soil at a site to be used for a septic drain field should preferably be impermeable.

B. The drain tiles in a septic drain field should be sloped at least 1/4 inch per foot.

C. The effluent sewage from a septic drain field may be permitted to flow to a potable water course.

D. Drain fields should be at least 100 feet from any surface water or well.

88. A parking area for a community college must accommodate 400 cars. What is the least amount of level land required for this parking area?

A. Two acres

B. Three acres

C. Four acres

D. Five acres

89. The contours shown represent a road

    I. with a crown at the center.

    II. with a gutter at the center.

    III. with a six-inch-high curb at each edge.

    IV. that is elevated six inches above the adjacent grade at each edge.

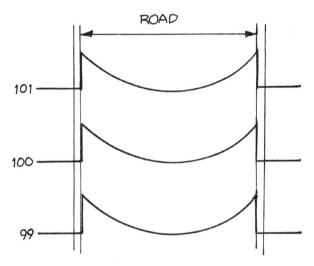

    A. I and III

    B. II and IV

    C. II and IV

    D. II and III

90. Place the following roadway types in order from smallest to largest based on their traffic carrying capacity.

    I.   Local access streets

    II. Collector streets

    III. Expressway

    IV. Arterial

    A. I, II, III, IV

    B. II, I, III, IV

    C. I, II, IV, III

    D. II, III, I, IV

91. An architect instructs his consulting civil engineer to ensure that the amount of soil removed from one portion of a site is equal to the amount added to another to avoid having to truck soil to or from the job site. This practice is called

    A. cutting the site.

    B. filling the site.

    C. balancing the site.

    D. engineering the site.

92. On a topographic survey, lines connecting points of equal elevation are called

    A. contour lines.

    B. property lines.

    C. fall lines.

    D. base lines.

93. Illustrated below is a proposed retaining wall superimposed on naturally sloping land. If the area on the west side of the wall were graded to a constant elevation of 4, what would be the elevation necessary at the highest point along the wall's top in order to retain the natural grade?

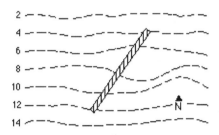

    A. 4 feet

    B. 8 feet

    C. 12 feet

    D. 16 feet

94. An ordinance in a small city prohibits new buildings from exceeding the height of the city hall dome, which is at elevation 168. For the construction of a new five-story office building along Main Street, between 1st Avenue and 2nd Avenue, which is the highest site that would comply with the ordinance assuming the owner requires a floor to floor height of 11 feet?

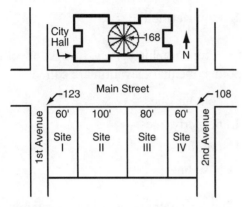

A. Site I

B. Site II

C. Site III

D. Site IV

95. In a structure located in the southwest desert area of the United States, which of the following design features would most significantly recognize the climatic problems of the area?

A. Insulated glass windows

B. Flat roof planes

C. Fixed vertical louvers

D. Deeply recessed openings

96. Construction within a flood plain is

A. never permitted.

B. limited to nonresidential uses.

C. usually uneconomical because the land can be used more efficiently for agriculture.

D. generally limited and elevated above flood level.

97. Select the correct statements about solar radiation.

I.   The south wall of a building receives maximum solar radiation in the winter.

II. The south wall of a building receives maximum solar radiation in the summer.

III. The roof and east and west walls of a building receive maximum solar radiation in the winter.

IV. The roof and east and west walls of a building receive maximum solar radiation in the summer.

A. I and III

B. I and IV

C. II and III

D. II and IV

98. The winter solstice refers to

A. the day when the length of day and night is equal.

B. the day that has the maximum hours of sunlight.

C. the day with the minimum hours of sunlight.

D. none of the above.

1. C and E. The correct answers are C and E. Large spaces used often by many people should be located on the ground floor, in a central location near the entrance (C) so that they are easy to find and use and circulation is minimal. It is also a good idea to make toilet rooms readily accessible (E) wherever large groups gather. At the extreme end (A) is likely too distant for easy access; on the second level (B) is unnecessarily inconvenient for senior citizens; and the best view (D) seems to be an unimportant feature for a meeting room.

2. B. The answer is *identify the nature of the problem.* The chief goal of the programming process is to identify and understand the nature of an architectural problem. Programming may establish desirable objectives (choice A), and it may also organize structural, aesthetic, and budgetary standards (choice C). However, since programming states, rather than solves, the problem, it does not determine form (choice D). Programming is clearly not design; it is the process of identifying essential information that permits one to create an intelligent and responsive design.

3. B. The answer is *the mortgagee may have greater difficulty in obtaining repayment.* A mortgage on a piece of property is a contract by which a buyer borrows money and pledges the property as security for the loan. Second mortgages are subordinate to first mortgages, that is, the holder of the first mortgage has first claim against the property. If the buyer defaults on a prior mortgage, the second mortgagee may pay the defaulted amount, add it to his loan, and foreclose on the property (choice A). The mortgagee may be an individual or an institution (choice C), and in any event, second mortgages are bound by all prevailing laws (choice D),

including those concerning usury, which is lending money at exorbitant rates. Higher interest on second mortgages is justified by the additional risk and difficulty one has in obtaining repayment on the loan, as described above (correct choice B).

4. B. The answer is *Two-person rectangular tables.* The differences in economy and comfort among the various choices is relatively minor; however, the differences in flexibility are significant. The least flexible seating arrangements are those that are fixed, such as counter seating (choice A) or booth seating (choice D). Between rectangular and found tables, rectangular are preferred, since they may be joined end to end to create a variety of groupings. Finally, two-person tables are most suitable, because the greatest flexibility is always achieved by using the smallest organizational unit.

5. B. All of the choices are features of prominent modern buildings and all apply to the John Hancock Building with the exception of B. The building, designed by Skidmore, Owings, and Merrill, is a single battered tower that inclines inward as it rises 100 stories above Michigan Avenue. It is set in a predominantly paved shopping plaza (not a park-like setting), and the tower is further distinguished by the exposed diagonal steel braces. Answer B, therefore, is the incorrect answer we are looking for.

6. A. The efficiency of a building is the ratio of the net area to the gross area, where the net area is the sum of all usable floor spaces not including circulation and general service areas. If we assign number 1 to the 65 percent efficient building and number 2 to the 70 percent efficient building, we have

$$\frac{\text{net area } 1}{\text{gross area } 1} = 0.65 \text{ and}$$

$$\frac{\text{net area 2}}{\text{gross area 2}} = 0.70$$

Since the net area remains constant,

net area 1 = 0.65 gross area 1 =
net area 2 = 0.70 gross area 2

0.65 gross area 1 = 0.70 gross area 2

$$\frac{\text{gross area 2}}{\text{gross area 1}} = \frac{0.65}{0.70} = 0.93$$

In other words, the gross area of the 70 percent efficient building is 93 percent of the gross area of the 65 percent efficient building. The gross area thus decreases by 7 percent (correct choice A).

7. **Humus.** Questions pertaining to landscaping may test the candidate's understanding of soils, soil improvement, fertilizers, and various organic and inorganic matter utilized in growing plant material. The definition provided refers to humus. In contrast, *mulch* is generally used to help conserve moisture, control temperature, prevent surface compaction, reduce runoff and erosion, improve soil structure, or control weeds. *Muck* is a combination of soil and water, having a higher mineral content than peat. It is decomposed to the point where the original plant parts cannot be identified. *Compost,* when mixed with nitrogen and soil, is used as an organic fertilizer. The principal purpose in making compost is to permit the organic materials to become crumbly and to reduce the carbon-nitrogen ratio of the material.

8. **C.** This type of question tests the candidate's understanding of the various components that make up a project budget. To begin with, one must be aware of the difference between a project development budget and a construction budget. The construction budget consists of the anticipated contract price plus a small contingency allowance for change orders and other costs incurred during construction. The project budget, however, includes not only the cost of construction, but in addition, all costs for fees, surveys, tests and inspections, utility connections, furnishings and equipment, etc. Those costs over and above the basic construction cost normally amount to about 15 percent of the total project budget. The efficiency of a building is the ratio of the net area to the gross area, where the net area is the total usable floor area, not including circulation and general service. Since we are told that the programmed net area is 49,000 square feet and the efficiency is to be 70 percent, we can calculate the building's gross area as follows: 49,000 ÷ 70% = 70,000 square feet. Consequently, choice A is a correct statement. To calculate the building's unit cost, we simply divide the cost of construction by the total building area. Since we know that the construction budget is about 85 percent of the 6.3 million dollar project budget, the unit cost is not $6,300,000 ÷ 70,000 SF, but roughly 85 percent of that, or about $76.50 per square foot. Choice B is therefore the incorrect statement and the correct answer to the question. The architect's fee is usually based on a percentage of the cost of construction; we can calculate this to be 8% × .85 × 6,300,000 = $428,400 (C is correct). And, as stated before, furnishings and equipment are included within a project budget; therefore, choice D is also a correct statement.

9. **B.** This question tests a candidate's knowledge about two basic considerations in the programming of lecture space: 1) the amount of area required to accommodate a specified number of occupants and, 2) the preferred shape of a space for a particular

programmed use. Fixed auditorium-type seating requires approximately seven square feet per occupant. Allowing for the additional 500 square feet of lecture and demonstration area at the front of the room, we calculate the space need to be 300 × 7 + 500 = 2,600 square feet. The shape of a lecture hall is determined largely by sight lines, since the demonstration table must be clearly visible from all seats. Consequently, a square room is not desirable, since some of its seats will be located too far to the sides of the room, causing distorted sight lines, especially for projected images on a screen. A narrow but deep rectangular shape will provide good sight lines for half the seats, but those located in the rear portion will be too far away to see and hear well. Choice A is too small a space, choice C is too large, and choice D is a poorly proportioned space. Choice B, however, is the correct size and a good proportion for the programmed use.

10. **Bubble diagram.** The bubble diagram, sometimes called a *programmatic diagram,* is a graphic tool that represents the relative relationships of program elements in order to communicate functional requirements and adjacencies.

11. **B.** We assume that "direct" refers to the circulation path to these elevators from any part of the ground floor. Therefore, we are looking for the diagram that places the tower centrally over the ground floor, so that access from any point is relatively equidistant. The correct solution is answer B, since the other diagrams show greater distances from the farthest ground floor points to the center of the tower.

12. **B.** The principal purpose of a diagrammatic layout is to determine graphically the functional relationships (V) among various programmed spaces.

A quick concept diagram shows each space as a rough shape with no regard to scale. These shapes are then connected by lines or arrows to other shapes with which they have a functional association. By so doing, one establishes not only a graphic indication of the functions, but also the important circulation relationships (II) that exist among the spaces. Thus, diagrammatic layouts deal with circulation and function, as stated in correct answer B. Bubble diagrams do not deal with areas (I), since they are not to scale; nor do they involve structure or form (III and IV), which are generally considered later in the design process.

13. **C.** In this question we must assume that complete satisfaction of the objective is impossible, since every side of the structure cannot be oriented toward the water. Therefore, the best solution will be the one that allows the greatest number of units to overlook the water. We should also assume that an authentic view is one that encompasses up to a 45 degree angle from any unit. In design A, exactly half of the units have a view of the water. By rotating the cruciform plan, as in design B, we have not materially changed the relationship of the units to the water; half of the units still have a view. In schematic designs C and D we have an L-shaped structure in which more units can be placed on one side of the corridor than the other. Therefore, the solution in which the long sides face the water (correct answer C) is the one in which the greatest possible number of units have a water view. In fact, design C provides a water view for more than half of the units, while design D provides a view for somewhat less than half of the units.

14. **C.** This question may seem abstract and esoteric. Nevertheless, questions of

this kind often appear on the exam, and candidates should be prepared for them. Programming is the process of searching for sufficient information about a proposed project, so that the problem can be stated (I and IV are correct). It involves functional solutions, while the design process involves actual physical solutions (II and III are incorrect).

15. **C.**   The floor area ratio (FAR) is the ratio of the total floor area of a building to the total area of the lot. The lot in this question has an area of $75 \times 150 = 11,250$ square feet. The total permitted floor area of a building on this lot is the floor area ratio of 2.0 multiplied by the lot area of 11,250 square feet, or 22,500 square feet (answer C). The front, rear, and side yards refer to required open space on all four sides of a building and are irrelevant in this question. The net floor area (D) is the total, or gross, floor area minus the area used for service and circulation, and is also irrelevant in this question.

16. **D.**   The building codes establish minimum allowable sizes for many building elements including stairways, corridors, toilet rooms, and mechanical spaces. The codes, therefore, have the second greatest impact on the size of a building other than the owner's program requirements.

17. **D.**   Questions on this exam may test your ability to read and comprehend bubble diagrams or diagrammatic layouts. In this question, there are several possible exit paths from the cafeteria. The most direct path is through the lobby and out to the entry plaza (A). Another possibility is through the lobby to the exit corridor, which leads outside (C). A third path is out to the dining terrace (B). Since no exit from electronic games is shown, this space would not be part of any exit path.

18. **Property tax.**   Property tax is a tax based on a property's value, as distinguished from a tax on income, personal possessions, or sales price. This tax was originally a general tax on land, buildings, and possessions, such as livestock and tools. However, possessions could easily be concealed when the tax assessor came around, and thus, it gradually became a tax on the physical property that was impossible to conceal or move elsewhere. The value that is taxed is not necessarily the property's market value, but only a valuation for tax purposes. Thus, valuations and/or tax rates may be raised or lowered in order to produce desired tax revenues.

19. **A.**   The answer is *an expression in which classic elements are used unconventionally.* Mannerism was a style of architecture in Italy and elsewhere that evolved between the Renaissance and baroque periods. The style was an expression of the manner, rather than the substance, of classical elements, and it was characterized by a lack of classical harmony and order, as well as the incongruous use of classical motifs (choice A). Principal examples of this style in Italy are Michelangelo's Medici Chapel and Laurentian Library. Some postmodernists have been likened to mannerists (choice C), because elements from the past may be used in unconventional ways in some of their buildings. An example of this are the classically inspired columns used by Charles Moore (choice D) in his own house in Orinda in 1961. Nevertheless, mannerism is not the same as postmodernism (choice C), nor is it a term that characterizes the work of Charles Moore (choice D).

20. **D.**   The answer is *highly irregular contours.* The cluster-type arrangement features a concentrated grouping of

residential units surrounded by open space. The idea of clustering is to place units in a tight group by reducing lot sizes, and thereby end up with large common areas of open space that can be developed or simply enjoyed in a communal way. In cluster plans, the lengths of streets and utility runs are generally reduced, and most residential units adjoin some open space. For these reasons, such a development is most suitable in a hilly area, an area defined by irregular contours. Clustered units may be sited on moderately sloping land, while more steeply sloping land could be left undeveloped as common open space. The other three choices have little relevance in the arrangement of residential units. The problems and influences of land size, natural foliage, and fuel costs are similar regardless of the development type.

21. **A.** The answer is *it restored human scale to the new industrial cities.* The City Beautiful Movement was an outgrowth of the enormous influence generated by the Chicago World's Fair of 1893. On the shores of Lake Michigan, Daniel Burnham created the spacious, classically-scaled White City, which launched a classic revival that swept the country (choice B). This surge of development led to the creation of city planning organizations (choice C), and resulted in a profusion of classically-inspired civic centers, dome-topped structures, and grand plazas, complete with monuments and fountains. Unfortunately, the scale of development, far from restoring a more human expression (choice A), promoted the monumental and grandiose.

22. **A.** Regarding circulation systems, there are several patterns that have developed through history to solve specific traffic problems. The curvilinear system (choice A), utilizes the natural topography by following the natural contour of the land as much as possible. In this regard there is less grading work required and the natural flow of water across a site would be less disturbed making it a good choice for sustainable design. The grid system usually consists of equally spaced streets which run perpendicular to each other. This system of circulation is most often used on flat land and ideally continues uninterrupted. The radial system directs flow to a common central point and in cases where there is a great deal of activity at the center, may cause congestion and crowding. Because of their rigid geometric patterns, both of these systems lack regard for the natural topography and create visual monotony (B and C are incorrect). The linear system of circulation, is typical of a highway, railway, or canal and is unsuitable for use in a community setting (D is incorrect).

23. **Catchment area.** The term *catchment area* describes the geographic area from where the participants in a particular activity are drawn. Catchments may be local, regional, or national. For example, Disneyland draws its visitors from all over the country, while a local shopping mall may only draw its visitors from surrounding neighborhoods.

24. **C.** All of the statements are true except C. The statement provided in C is true of deciduous trees, which lose their leaves in the winter months, but not coniferous trees. Therefore, C is the incorrect answer we are looking for.

25. **A.** Vandalism, which is the willful destruction of property, is an unfortunate fact of modern life, and a subject with which architects must often be concerned. To deal with the perils of vandalism, one must understand the techniques of

security. For example, at exterior spaces the key technique is surveillance, with local residents taking the responsibility over their own locality. In this regard one would arrange paths for high visibility (A is correct), and provide well-lighted grounds (C is incorrect). Further, one would avoid curved paths (B is incorrect) because they tend to obscure the view ahead. Finally, one must be realistic. While attractive or natural materials are desirable, they are not immune to vandalism and durability is a more critical quality (D is incorrect).

26. **C.**   Architectural symbolism has existed and been employed for thousands of years. Throughout nearly all that time, informal or casual arrangements have signified relative unimportance, while importance has been characterized by rigid formality. In the case of an important public building, therefore, the designer would include a symmetrical arrangement (II), which is regarded as formal, and a long flight of entrance steps (III), which accentuates the insignificance of the user, and thus, the relative importance of the institution. Additionally, one would use a flagpole (V), since this object symbolizes the institution's important association with the governing state or country. The use of many entrance doors (I) actually diminishes the importance of a single principal entrance; furthermore, a tall, rather than wide door would signify greater prominence. Finally, for the reasons already mentioned, one would avoid random placement of openings (IV). The correct combination is found in answer C.

27. **B.**   Buildings that disregard the sun's impact frequently require large amounts of energy to heat and cool. When determining a building's shape, designers should consider the solar orientation that will minimize the use of energy. In general, the optimum shape of a building is one that loses a minimum amount of heat in the winter and gains a minimum amount of heat in the summer. Considering the choices of this question, a circular or square shape (I and II) are not desirable, since they have the least amount of enclosing walls for the area. This means that sunlight will strike an absolute minimum amount of exterior surface. The very best shape is a form elongated in the east-west direction (not the north-south as stated in III), as this form will derive maximum heat gain during the winter months, while exposing the shorter east and west sides to minimum heat gain in the summer. Staggered or stacked buildings (IV and V) can also be beneficial, since direct sunlight will strike large surface areas, especially if the building's longer dimensions are oriented to the south. The correct combination of choices is found in correct answer B.

28. **B.**   A path is a circulation route, such as a street or a highway. A district is a section of a city that has an identifying character, such as a neighborhood, a suburb, or a college campus. An edge is the boundary between districts, such as a shore line, a railroad line, or a wall of buildings. A landmark is a prominent visual feature that acts as a point of reference, such as a major department store, a city hall, or a train station. A node is a center of activity, such as a square, a plaza, or a civic center. Although the university campus in this question might be considered a landmark or a node, it is primarily a district (correct answer B).

29. **C.**   The Second Empire Style, named for the Second French Empire, was popular throughout the Western world in the mid- to late-19th century. It had two features that were clearly identifiable: the mansard

roof (I) and the pavilion, which consisted of one or more forward breaks in elevation (III). These were generally symmetrical and at the center although they could also be at other locations as well. This style was widely used in governmental and other buildings to convey an image of prestige and authority.

30. **A.** Spread footings (B) are appropriate where good soils are found at a shallow depth. Since the site in this question is underlain by 20 feet of loose fill, spread footings would be inappropriate. Placing spread footings on recompacted fill (C) is often economical where the maximum depth of fill is about five feet, and would therefore be uneconomical in this case. A mat foundation (D), which is essentially one large footing under the entire building, is sometimes used where soil conditions are fair to poor. But since we have no information about the loose fill close to the surface, we cannot assume that it would be adequate to support building loads. A better solution would be grade beams supported on piles that extend into the sand layer (correct choice A).

31. **B.** Symmetry is a balanced arrangement of elements that are exactly the same on each side of a central axis. Symmetry is found throughout nature, and has become associated in the man-made environment with formality and authority (I and III). Symmetry is most appropriate where building programs are uncomplicated (II) and building sites are regular in shape (IV is incorrect).

32. **B.** Removing vehicular traffic from the interior of a large residential project may be a desirable goal, since it allows the interior to be used for recreation. However, such developments often have more crime than comparable projects having streets that continue through the site (I is incorrect, II is correct). The reason is that through streets are easily patrolled and provide more direct access and the likely presence of people. Symbolic barriers, such as planters, low walls, and formal entries do not physically restrict criminal activity, but tend to inhibit such activities by making potential criminals more conspicuous (III is correct). Play areas should be located relatively close to homes, where they can be watched by residents. Locating such areas far from dwelling units invites vandalism and possibly more serious crimes (IV is incorrect). The correct choices are therefore II and III (answer B).

33. **B.** A rectangular box with its long axis in the east-west direction is the most appropriate for a temperate climate, in which there is too much heat in the summer and not enough heat in the winter. The long east-west axis provides a great deal of southern exposure and a minimum of eastern and western exposure. This is best in winter, when the predominant heat gain is on the south facade. Conversely, in the summer, the primary gain is on the roof and on the east and west facades, which are minimal in a building with a long east-west axis.

34. **B.** The answer is *two*. A candidate must know two facts to solve this problem: the definition of FAR and the number of square feet in an acre. FAR, or floor area ratio, is the ratio between the gross floor area of a building and the gross land area on which the building sits. In this case, the gross floor area of the building is 17,420 square feet on each of five floors, or $17,420 \times 5 = 87,100$ square feet. The gross land area is one acre, which contains 43,560 square feet. The FAR, therefore, is $87,100 / 43,560 = 1.999$. Note that in calculating FAR ratios, gross

areas are always used, with no regard for elements such as building circulation or site setbacks.

35. D.   The correct answer is *None of the above*. Choice I is not correct. The zone of the earth that supports human life is an extremely fragile ecosystem. This biosphere, which has evolved over millions of years, has been dramatically affected by the growth of human activity in the last 100 years. While innovative technologies are improving energy efficiency of some building systems, the vast majority of the built environment is energy inefficient (choice II is incorrect). Toxic substances have the tendency to expand and affect large areas. For example, the air above the Great Lakes contains evidence of DDT, a toxic pesticide banned in the United States decades ago. It was discovered that DDT is captured in the jet stream bringing toxic materials from far away continents that still use the pesticides (choice III is incorrect). Finally, while recycling is helpful, it is just the beginning of the sustainable design process. The principals of sustainable design say that we need to have more building products that can be recycled and are biodegradable to create a more sustainable ecosystem.

36. C.   Life-cycle costs include construction costs (around 15 percent), as well as operational and maintenance costs, taxes, financing, replacement, and renovation (B and D are correct). Financing costs may be decreased if the design and construction processes are accelerated using fast-track or other similar delivery systems (A is correct). C is the incorrect statement we are looking for; although high quality products have a greater initial cost, they generally require less maintenance and have a longer life span than lower quality products, resulting in a lower long-term cost.

37. A, B, and D.   All provided answers are correct with the exception of C. Deteriorated architectural features shall be replaced rather than repaired, wherever possible, with materials that match the design, color, texture, and other visual qualities of the original materials. All guidelines presented are accurate, with the exception of the matter in which deteriorated architectural features are dealt with. These should be repaired, whenever possible, in preference to their replacement. If repair is not feasible or architectural features are missing, their replacement should be based on accurate duplications that are substantiated by historical evidence.

38. B.   The answer is *the total number of occupants in the building*. The total width of required exits is determined by the total occupant load of a particular floor plus an additional allowance for occupants of floors above and below that floor, if those occupants use the same exit path. The required width is usually calculated by dividing the total number of occupants by a factor, such as 50, resulting in a total exit width expressed in feet. For example, if the total occupant load of a building was 600, the total width of required exits would be 600/50 = 12 feet of width. This width would be divided approximately equally among four separate exits (three-foot-wide doors). The total exit width has nothing to do with floor area, nor does it depend on building usage, although the floor area per occupant may be specified by usage in the code.

39. C.   Candidates are expected to understand the theory and application of building code regulations. Although all building codes used in this country are generally similar, they are by no means identical. The code most frequently used as the basis for questions on the licensing exams is the International Building Code. According to this code, every building is classified by the building official according to its use or character of its occupancy (III) and its type of construction (II), making C the correct answer.

40. **D.**   Candidates often find it difficult to differentiate between a building code and a zoning ordinance. The primary purpose of the building code is to provide for the safety and health of the public. It is created by an ordinance to regulate the construction of buildings within a municipality. In contrast, zoning is created by an ordinance to regulate the character and use of a parcel of land. Zoning ordinances stipulate the type of development; i.e., residential, commercial, industrial, agricultural, and so forth, that may take place within a given area. In most instances, zoning ordinances also control the extent of allowable land coverage, setbacks from property lines, allowable densities, and building heights and areas. Building codes also regulate maximum building heights, areas, and allowable number of stories. However, these limitations are based on construction and occupancy types to provide for the safety of the public. Similar restrictions imposed under zoning ordinances are intended to provide uniform standards of development to protect the environment and property values. The correct answer is D.

41. **A.**   Most authorities agree that the goal of barrier-free design is to permit any person with a handicap to participate in normal activities without help—in other words, autonomous functioning (correct answer A). This includes not only the non-

ambulatory (B), but also the ambulatory who are handicapped, such as the blind. Choices C and D are also correct, as far as they go, but they are incomplete. Physical barriers must be eliminated outside of, as well as within, all buildings (C). And finally, unobstructed access (D) serves little purpose if the handicapped person cannot use the facilities once he arrives at his destination. Candidates should note that in this question, where each choice is partially correct, the right answer is the choice that is most inclusive. In other words, some questions require one to find the answer that is most correct and, therefore, better than all the others.

42. **C.**   All of the statements concerning barrier-free design are true, with the exception of correct answer C. An unresolved problem exists with handicapped individuals in the event of fire in a multistoried building. In that case, the able-bodied will exit through enclosed fire-stair towers. The handicapped, however, must rely on elevators, which are risky because they tend to stall at the fire floor; on aid from the able-bodied, which is unpredictable; or on "refuge" compartments at each floor, which are designed to provide protection long enough to allow the fire to be extinguished. All of these alternatives have drawbacks and create a serious problem of life safety that barrier-free design has yet to solve. Concerning choice B, it is true that all building users benefit from certain barrier-free elements that are provided expressly for the handicapped. For example, nearly all able-bodied individuals would appreciate ramps rather than steps, door levers rather than knobs, wider entrances, non-slip floors, and a general absence of hazardous building elements. Incidentally, choice D states that project costs increase with the

inclusion of handicapped provisions, which is true, but the increase rarely exceeds 2 percent, on the average, of the total project budget.

43. **D.**   All of the features listed should be incorporated when providing barrier-free phones, with the exception of I. Telephones need not be placed on the ground floor because all other floors must also be handicapped accessible. Further, phones must be provided in locations where doors comply with code requirements to provide access to those in wheelchairs (answer III). All other choices are standard practice to meet the requirements of barrier-fee design as expressed in correct answer D.

44. **A.**   Knurled door knobs are those that have a series of small ridges carved around their edges. They are used principally to identify hazardous areas to those who are visually handicapped (correct answer A) and, thus, cannot be warned by other means. A blind person touching the knurled surface is alerted to the fact that beyond the door may lie a boiler room, fire escape, loading platform, or other area that is a hazard to one who is unable to see. For this same purpose, square knobs are sometimes used, as well as knurled levers, etc.

45. **B.**   Eminent domain is the right of the government to take private property for public use, with the owner receiving fair compensation. Ordinarily, a governmental agency will first attempt to buy the land in the normal manner, negotiating the price with the owner, rather than exercise its right of eminent domain (incorrect statements III and IV). If agreement with the owner cannot be reached, eminent domain may be used as a last resort (I and II). In that case, the value of the property may have to be determined by the court (V). Since

statements I and II are correct, B is the answer to this question.

46. **Setbacks.**   The primary purpose of setbacks is to provide light, air, and spaciousness to surrounding properties. Although setbacks may be used to provide off-street parking or fire-fighting access, neither of these is the principal purpose of setbacks.

47. **D.**   Zoning ordinances sometimes cause undue hardship to owners of specific parcels of land. Exceptions to or deviations from the precise terms of the zoning ordinances are sometimes permitted, and these are called zoning variances (correct answer D). Spot zoning (A) is the zoning of a parcel of land to permit a use different from that of the surrounding area. Incentive zoning (B) permits certain zoning requirements to be waived if the developer of the parcel provides special features, for example, allowing a greater floor area in exchange for the developer providing an open plaza. A conditional use (C) may be permitted if specific conditions are met and it is in the public interest, such as a neighborhood school in a residential zone.

48. **C.**   The sketch on the next page will clarify this problem. The eave projects 6 feet beyond the building, of which 1'-6" is permitted to extend past the setback. Thus, the building must be at least 4'-6" (6'-0" minus 1'-6") inside of the side yard. Since the setback is 6 feet, the building must be no closer than 10'-6" (6'-0" plus 4'-6") from the property line.

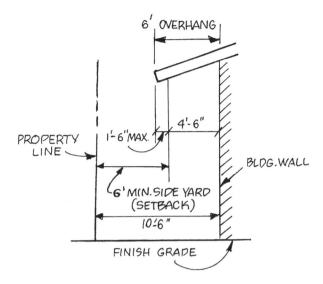

49. Spot zoning.   A zoning ordinance is a law enacted by a municipality for the general welfare, which establishes zones or districts within which the location, height, and use of buildings are regulated. If a building already exists when a zoning ordinance is enacted, its lawful use may usually be continued even though it does not conform with the zoning regulations. This is known as a *nonconforming use.* Sometimes, small spot zones are established. Spot zones are sometimes inconsistent with the general intent of the zoning regulations and which favor a particular property owner.

50. B.   A zoning ordinance is a law enacted by a municipality for the general welfare, which establishes zones or districts, within which the location, height, and use of buildings are regulated. Each of the four choices represents a deviation from normal zoning regulations. If a building already exists when a zoning ordinance is enacted, its lawful use may usually be continued even though it does not conform with the zoning regulations. This is known as a nonconforming use (D is incorrect). Where strict application of zoning regulations would result in exceptional hardship, special permission to deviate from the regulations

may be granted. Such permission is called a variance (B is correct). A conditional use is similar to a variance, except that it permits a special use, such as a school or hospital, which is for the public welfare and convenience (C is incorrect). Sometimes, small spot zones are established, which may be inconsistent with the general intent of the zoning regulations and which favor a particular property owner (A is incorrect).

51. Easement.   An easement allows a property owner to use the property of another for a specific use. Common types of easements include the right of a public utility to gain access to private land for the purpose of placing and maintaining utility services. Easements exist for other reasons, such as to gain access such as for a shared driveway. *Covenants* are restrictions placed on a property to protect the aesthetic harmony and value of properties. *Deeds* are documents conveying property from one owner to another.

52. D.   This question simply tests a candidate's ability to use the table provided in the building code. We are told that the building's Use Group is B, and the Construction Type is IV. Locating these two criteria to the left and top of the table, we simply read down to the appropriate square that indicates the maximum permitted number of stories (4) and the maximum permitted area per floor (18,000). The correct answer, therefore, is D.

53. X̶.D. Office (O) is not a recognized Use Group, rather offices and several other uses are placed in the common classification "Business" (D is incorrect). Institutional and Assembly are both classifications that are recognized by the Building Code.

54. C.   All of the choices provided are benefits of the fire resistance requirements, however, only choice C is the primary purpose of these requirements. In general, the building code is not as concerned with protecting the structure and its contents as it is with protecting the lives of a building's occupants.

55. **B.**   Linking the total floor area, irrespective of the number of stories, to the lot area is known as the floor area ratio (FAR) (B is correct). This limits the overall bulk of a building without dictating what form it must take. Allowable floor area is a term used in the building code and is an absolute maximum (A is incorrect). Required yards are distances that must be maintained from the property line to the structure (C is incorrect). Maximum lot coverage is a maximum percentage that may be covered by all surfaces including buildings, parking, sidewalks, etc. (D is incorrect).

56. **A.**   The requirements for building exiting are based upon calculations and requirements as set forth in the building code (A is correct). The code does not allow the architect, the owner, or precedent to establish different expected occupancy rates for the purposes of establishing exit sizes.

57. **D.**   In stairways that serve as required building exits, all of the items listed are regulated by the building code (D is correct). In addition, the flame-spread ratings and smoke ratings of finish materials, lighting, and ventilation requirements are all governed by the building code.

58. **B.**   The answer is 1-3-4. A critical path diagram indicates the order in which various operations comprising a project are to be accomplished. Each even has a start and finish, represented by circles, and

referred to by a number. Between events are letters representing activities and below the letters are numbers representing the number of days each activity is estimated to take. Since each path of a diagram must be traversed to complete the project, the total project time is established by the path with the greatest amount of total time. This is known as the critical path. In the network diagram of this problem, the critical path is 1-3-4, with a total time of $4 + 2 = 6$ days. The path of choice A is 3 days, choice C is $1 + 3 = 4$ days, and choice D is $1 + 2 + 2 = 5$ days.

59. **A.**   Critical path method (CPM) is a management tool used in the planning and scheduling of construction, in which a construction project is divided into separate identifiable jobs, called activities. These are indicated graphically on a network diagram, including the estimated time to complete each activity. Float time is the extra time available for an activity or group of activities above its estimated time duration without any resulting delay in completion of the project. A is therefore the correct answer.

60. **D.**   This type of question tests the candidate's ability to use his judgment in situations where financing dictates cost, scope, and quality of a project. It would be presumptuous on the architect's part to recommend a 25 percent increase in student fees (A). Such an action would require the approval of the college's administration and student body—a policy matter with which the architect should not concern himself. Delaying the project (B) would almost certainly result in an escalation of cost and an increased budget. Furthermore, the architect is not qualified to project future student enrollments and would, once again, be acting outside his area of expertise.

Proceeding with a project for which adequate funds are not on hand (C) is unrealistic. The architect cannot arbitrarily reduce space needs 25 percent, nor can he reasonably expect to reduce the project's quality 25 percent. The only reasonable course of action is to convince the owner to reduce his overall space needs to meet the budget prior to entering into an agreement (D), and to attempt to develop efficient uses of space that will satisfy the users' functional needs. The correct answer is D.

61. **A.** A construction loan is short-term interim financing, which is in effect during the construction of a project. For smaller projects, construction loans are often made through banks or savings and loan associations rather than mortgage brokers, because this procedure is usually less costly and time consuming. Regardless of who the lender is, the borrower must pay certain fees at the time he obtains the loan, including the discount, legal fees, and recording fees. The discount (A) may be known by various names—loan placement charge, origination fee, "points"—and represents a fee charged by the lender to the borrower for the privilege of obtaining the loan. For example, if the lender states that the discount will be two points, that means that for every $1,000 borrowed, the borrower will actually receive only $980, the difference of $20 being two points (i.e., 2 percent) of the $1,000 borrowed. But the borrower will have to repay the full $1,000, plus the interest on $1,000. In effect, this raises the true interest rate paid by the borrower. The lender's justification for the origination fee is that it is required to pay the costs of the loan officer as well as other loan processing costs. Recording fees (B) include charges made by the county to record the mortgage, as well as any taxes levied by the state and federal government

on the transaction. A balloon payment (C) is a final mortgage payment that is much larger than the typical periodic payments. And finally amortization (D) refers to the payment of a debt in periodic installments. The correct answer is A.

62. **A.** CPM is a planning and scheduling technique that uses network diagrams, not bar graphs, to show various construction activities and how they are related sequentially (III is incorrect). I and II are correct: the critical path is that path of construction activities that requires the greatest amount of time. Other paths, called float paths, require less time. The difference in required time between the critical path and any other path is call the float for that path.

63. **C.** The critical path method (CPM) is a system of scheduling construction operations where each activity is assigned a start date, duration, and an end date. In addition, activities are linked to indicate instances when one activity must be complete before the next activity may start. These relationships are shown in network diagrams. The resulting shortest path to completion is known as the critical path (C is correct).

64. **A.** Programming, while a vital part of the planning process, is not considered part of an architect's basic services. AIA contract documents recognize that the owner is expected to begin the design process with an established program. Many architects can, and should, assist the owner with this phase, however it is generally recognized as being an "additional service" for which the architect is entitled to additional compensation.

65. **A.** The critical path is the one in the network diagram that requires the greatest

amount of time to complete. In this case, path 1-3-4-5 requires 14 days, whereas 1-4-5 requires 7 days, and 1-2-3-4-5, 13 days. Path 1-2-3-4 is not actually a critical path, since it does not include activity 5.

66. D.   All of the factors indicated will have some effect on the time required, however the size of the design team should have the least impact (D is correct). If the team is well balanced, if they work well together, if they are skilled and experienced, and if they can communicate readily with the client, then the size of the team should not have a significant effect.

67. D.   Choice D is the incorrect answer. Float time is the difference in time duration between the critical path and any other path, therefore it is a measure of extra time available for a given activity (A and B are correct). As long as the float time is not exceeded, no delay in project completion will result (C is correct). This is true so long as the delay is not in the critical path. By definition, those activities in the critical path do not have float and therefore may not be delayed without impact to the project schedule (D is incorrect).

68. C.   Governmental jurisdictions frequently finance large construction projects through the sale of general obligation bonds (C is correct). In the United States, property taxes are primarily used for schools and core government services such as police and fire protection. Comprehensive planning and eminent domain are not financing methods.

69. D.   The construction documents phase is the phase of the project where final calculations and detailed layouts are performed. During design development, preliminary collations and layouts are

performed, however, ductwork design would be limited to single line layouts.

70. A.   The answer is *minimizes the amount of grading required to fit the building to the site.* Building on a level site is easier, more flexible, and less expensive than building on a sloping site. However, most sites do slope. By orienting a building's long dimension parallel to the contours, less earth is removed in the building's short direction when fitting the building to the site. Such grading has little effect on natural drainage (choice B), nor does it affect the available area for construction (choice C), which is more a matter of lot size. Solar orientation (choice D), has no bearing on the direction of contours.

71. C.   The answer is *150*. The gradient, or slope, or a road is calculated by the formula $G = V/H$, where G is the gradient, V is the vertical rise, and H is the horizontal distance in which the rise takes place. To find the vertical rise, solve for $V = G \times H$. Thus, $V = 0.05 \times 150 = 7.5$ feet, which is the total difference in elevation over the 150-foot distance. Uphill from elevation 142.5, therefore, the elevation will be 142.5 + 7.5, or 150.

72. A.   The answer is *more expensive than for a level site, because the line requires more sewer manholes.* Steep and irregular land is invariably more expensive to develop than level land, and underground sewer line installation is only one reason. Such land requires more sewer manholes (choice A) because a manhole is required wherever there is a change in the line's direction. Choices B and C use similar reasoning; lines that follow the ground's natural downward slope will save excavation costs. However, underground utilities must be run to where they are needed, which is not always in the downhill direction.

In addition, if sewers below street level require pumping stations to connect lines to mains in the street, the overall cost will rise substantially. Finally, the expense of installing underground utilities on sloping land exceeds that of level land (choice D), because of generally increased excavation, length of runs, and number of direction changes in the line.

73. C. The answer is *I, II, and V.* Contours are lines that connect points of equal elevation (I). Those that are solid represent proposed modifications to the existing landform (II), while dashed lines are used to represent existing or natural topography (III is incorrect). Although contour lines may close on themselves (IV is incorrect), for example, when indicating a summit or a depression, they may never split in two (V), since this would indicate an implausible topographic configuration.

74. D. The usual topographic map shows the location, size, and shape of physical and other features of a piece of land, including property lines, easements, and utilities (A); natural features, such as streams (B); man-made features, such as roads and buildings (C); and contours indicating elevation. Soil conditions, however, are not generally shown on a topographic map (correct answer D).

75. B. The answer is *I, II, and IV.* The hot-arid zone of the United States includes most of the southwest, from Texas and New Mexico west to the Southern California deserts. The region is characterized by clear skies, dry air, long periods of heat, and large variations in daily temperatures. In such a climate one would use thick walls (I), which tend to make interior spaces cooler by day and warmer at night by absorbing and then radiating the sun's heat. Wide overhangs (II) block the high summer

sun, and high ceilings (IV) allow a greater volume of space for air to circulate. Dense windbreaks (III) are generally unnecessary, since unpleasant winds are infrequent, being more closely associated with hot-humid, as well as cool, climactic zones.

76. A. The answer is *of frost and heaving of the subsoil.* If any of the other choices had occurred, the land beneath the paving would have settled, not risen. Filled land, insufficiently compacted soil, and broken pipes would all cause the soil to sink. Only the penetration of frost and ice would cause the subsoil to heave and the paving to rise above its original level.

77. D. We determine the ground slope by dividing the vertical change in height by the horizontal distance (G = V/H). 5% = 1 foot/H, or H = 1 foot/.05 = 20 feet.

78. C. Many candidates find it confusing to analyze the slope of the ground. However, it is important to be able to utilize the topography of a site in order to maximize the use of available land, both in site planning and building design. Grades for existing as well as man-made slopes are established by measuring the distance between contours at a given scale and a given contour interval. The formula is % grade = change in vertical elevation/horizontal distance × 100. Therefore, in the graded bank we are shown a four-foot change in elevation for every five horizontal feet of land. Using the formula we calculate as follows: 4/5 × 100 = 80%. The correct answer is C.

79. B. Vehicles entering a parking lot from the street are invariably traveling at a faster rate than those exiting (correct answer B), since they are in the process of slowing down from normal street speeds. Those exiting are moving along a restricted aisle width and are, therefore, traveling more slowly. In addition, vehicles exiting generally slow or even stop completely when they approach the street. This slower speed enables a driver to turn within a radius somewhat smaller than one traveling at a greater speed.

80. **C.**   All of the statements are true with the exception of correct answer C. Angled parking nearly always leads to more rapid traffic flow than perpendicular parking, because one can pull in and out of an angled space more quickly; hence, traffic is obstructed or halted for a shorter period of time. Concerning choice A, traffic aisles generally lead toward buildings so that the buildings are more visible, and customers can walk along traffic aisles instead of between cars.

81. **A.**   The U.S. System, which is the basis for much of the legal description of non-urban areas outside the original 13 states, established a grid of north-south lines (meridians) and east-west lines (parallels), which are 24 miles apart in each direction. Each 24-mile-square area is in turn divided into 16 townships, each six miles square. Each township is further divided into 36 square sections, each containing one square mile. Metes and bounds descriptions start at a point on the property boundary and then describe the length and direction of each boundary line in narrative form. Urban land is generally described by lot number, block name or number, and tract name or number.

82. **Deed restriction.**   A deed restriction is any clause in a deed that places limitations or restrictions on the use of the property.

83. **D.**   Utility lines that do not flow by gravity, but are under pressure and flow full, include water and gas lines (III and IV). Sanitary sewers and storm drains (I

and II) typically flow by gravity and flow only partially full.

84. **A.**   A swale is a flow path similar to a valley, in which the contours point uphill (correct answer A). A ridge is the reverse of a swale and is represented by contours that point downhill (B is incorrect). A trench drain is a device used to collect water before conducting it to underground pipes, while a drain pipe is any pipe used to carry water from collection points to disposal areas (C and D are incorrect).

85. **C.**   The grade of a slope is equal to the vertical rise divided by the horizontal distance, multiplied by 100 to convert it to a percentage. In this case, the vertical rise is $20 - 16 = 4$ feet, and the horizontal distance is 8 feet. The grade is therefore $4 \div 8 = 0.50 \times 100 = 50$ percent.

86. **B.**   The shape of the ground surface is most often shown on drawings by means of contours, which are imaginary lines that connect all points of equal elevation. A uniform slope is indicted by evenly-spaced parallel contours. A concave slope is indicated by parallel contours spaced closer together going uphill, as in this question. Parallel contours spaced farther apart going uphill indicate a convex slope, and contours which point uphill indicate a valley. If you find it hard to remember these typical contour characteristics, you can cut a section perpendicular to the contours, which in this case would look approximately like the curve shown below (a concave slope).

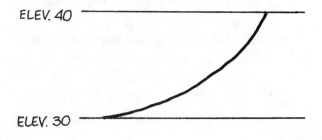

87. D. Where the soil is relatively pervious (A is incorrect), a septic tank that discharges into an underground drain field may provide an adequate sewage system. In that case, potential health hazards and water pollution must be considered (C is incorrect, D is correct). The tiles comprising the drain field should be placed at a very gentle slope of about 1 inch in 24 feet, or 1/24 inch per foot (B is incorrect).

88. B. Approximately 300 to 400 square feet per car is required for parking, including stalls and aisles. Therefore, the required area varies from 400 cars × 300 square feet per car, or 120,000 square feet to 400 × 400, or 160,000 square feet. Since there are 43,560 square feet in an acre, this converts to 120,000 ÷ 43,560 = 2.75 acres, and 160,000 ÷ 43,560 = 3.67 acres. Therefore, the least area required is about 2.75 acres. B, *3 acres,* is therefore the best answer.

89. A. If you cut a section through the road where the 100 contour meets the edges of the road, it will look like the sketch below. Therefore, there is a crown at the center of the road (I) and 6-inch-high curb at each edge (III).

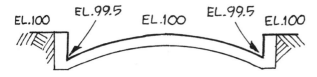

90. C. Local access streets provide access to low-intensity fronting them such as houses and often take the form of loops and cul-de-sacs. Collector streets serve as the transition between arterials and the local access streets. Although intersections with arterials may be controlled with traffic signals, intersections with local streets may have only stop signs. Arterial streets are continuous vehicular channels that connect with expressways by means of on and off ramps. They are typically two or more lanes wide in each direction. Expressways are designed to allow movement of large volumes of traffic between, around, and through urban centers. Vehicles move at more rapid speeds because access to and access from expressways is limited. Answer C is the correct answer.

91. C. In an ideal situation, a civil engineer will try to ensure that the amount of soil removed and added to different areas of a site is equal so that additional soil does not need to be imported or exported from the job site. This practice is called balancing the site (C is correct) and is desirable because trucking large quantities of soil can be expensive. Cutting the site is the process of removing soil (A is incorrect). Filling the site is the process of adding soil (B is incorrect). Engineering describes, in general terms, the role of the civil engineer (D is incorrect).

92. A. Lines that connect points of equal elevations are contour lines (A is correct). The other choices are lines that may be found on various types of site drawings, but they are not related to elevations or topography.

93. C. The answer is *12 feet.* What may appear at first to be confusing is actually a simple problem. There is only one factor to consider: Since the south end of the wall terminates at elevation 12, the wall must extend to that elevation in order to retain the earth at the east side of the wall, irrespective of the elevation of the level area at the west side. The high end of the wall would extend 8 feet above the adjacent grade at the west (12 − 4 = 8), and the elevation at the top of the wall would be 12 feet, or perhaps a few inches higher. Incidentally, the angle between the wall and existing contours is irrelevant.

94. C.   The answer is *site III*. By adding the widths of the sites along Main Street, we determine that the block between 1st and 2nd Avenues is 300 feet long. Since Main Street slopes 15 feet downward along its length, from 123 to 108, the slope is calculated to be 15/300 = .05, or an assumed uniform slope of 5 percent. Using this slope and moving eastward from the corner at 1st Avenue, the elevations at each of the site corners along Main Street are 123, 120, 115, 111, and 108 at the 2nd Avenue corner. Therefore, with 11-foot stories, the building height would be 11 × 5 = 55 feet. In order not to exceed the City Hall dome elevation of 168 feet, the ground floor elevation of the new 55-foot structure would have to be at 168 − 55 = 113, which is the exact midpoint of Site III. If one assumed eight-foot ceilings, Site III would still be the appropriate choice. Building on Site IV would comply with the ordinance, but it is not the highest site, while a five-story building on either Site I or Site II would exceed the City Hall dome elevation.

95. D.   The southwest desert location implies that the overwhelming climatic problem in the structure is solar heat gain. In this regard, we can eliminate the flat roof feature (B), since roof shape alone has little effect in reducing heat gain. Insulated glass (A) windows are helpful, and this is a possible answer. Fixed vertical louvers (C), especially on the south side of a building, do little to diminish direct solar heat gain when the sun is high. Horizontal louvers would be more efficient, but that is not one of our choices. Finally, deeply recessed openings (D) are very effective in shading glass, regardless of their orientation. In a choice between insulated glass and shaded glass, shaded glass (correct answer D) is preferred because preventing sun from reaching the glass is always more effective in reducing solar heat gain than controlling the gain once the glass has been exposed to sun.

96. D.   A flood plain is the relatively flat land within which a stream flows. When the volume of flow exceeds the stream's capacity, which occurs more or less regularly, it overflows its banks and spreads over the flood plain. Consequently, a flood plain should preferably be limited to uses such as agriculture or recreation. In practice, however, this is not always the case (A is incorrect) because of economic pressure to use the land for construction, rather than for agriculture or recreation (C is incorrect). Limited low-density housing is often permitted (B is incorrect), provided the structures are elevated above flood level (D is correct).

97. B.   By studying a sun chart for a location in the north temperate zone, which includes the United States, one can see that in the winter, the sun is low and oriented to the south. Therefore, the south wall of a building receives a great amount of solar radiation (I is correct), while the east and west walls and roof receive very little (III is incorrect). In the summer, the sun is higher and oriented more to the east and west. Therefore, the south wall receives less solar radiation (II is incorrect), while the east and west walls and roof receive more (IV is correct).

98. C.   The winter solstice refers to the day with the minimum hours of sunlight, which usually occurs on December 21 in the northern hemisphere (C is correct). Choice A describes both the autumn and spring equinox, which occur around September 21 and March 21 respectively. Choice B describes the summer solstice, which usually occurs on June 21. Therefore, C is the correct answer.